PERSPECTIVES ON

The
Triangle Shirtwaist
Factory Fire
Its Legacy of Labor Rights

KATIE MARSICO

mc **Marshall Cavendish**
Benchmark
New York

Marshall Cavendish Benchmark
99 White Plains Road
Tarrytown, NY 10591-5502
www.marshallcavendish.us

Expert Reader: Richard Greenwald, Dean, The Casperson School of Graduate
Studies, Drew University, Madison, New Jersey

All Internet sites were correct and addresses accurate at the time of printing.

Library of Congress Cataloging-in-Publication Data

Marsico, Katie, 1980–
The Triangle Shirtwaist Factory fire : its legacy of labor rights / by
Katie Marsico.
p. cm. — (Perspectives on)
Includes bibliographical references and index.
Summary: "Provides comprehensive information on industry and immigration,
the Triangle Shirtwaist Factory Fire, its aftermath, and labor rights"—Provided
by publisher.
ISBN 978-0-7614-4027-7
1. Triangle Shirtwaist Company—Fire, 1911—Juvenile literature. 2. New
York (N.Y.)—History—1898-1951—Juvenile literature. 3. Fires—New York
(State)—New York—History—20th century—Juvenile literature. 4. Clothing
factories—New York (State)—New York—Safety measures—History—20th
century—Juvenile literature. 5. Labor laws and legislation—New York
(State)—New York—History—20th century—Juvenile literature. I. Title.
F128.5.M123 2010
974.7′1041—dc22
2008023267

Editor: Christine Florie
Publisher: Michelle Bisson
Art Director: Anahid Hamparian
Series Designer: Sonia Chaghatzbanian

Photo research by Marybeth Kavanagh

Cover photo by AP Photo

The photographs in this book are used by permission and through the courtesy of:
The Granger Collection, New York: 3, 34, 38, 59; *Brown Brothers*, Sterling, PA: 8,
13, 25, 56; *The Art Archive/*Culver Pictures: 17; *AP Photo*: 30; Underwood &
Underwood/*Corbis*: 37; Bettmann/*Corbis*: 41, 47, 66; *AP Photo/*National Archives:
43; *AP Photo/*Kathy Willens: 70; Sukree Sukplang/Reuters/*Corbis*: 76; James
Leynse/*Corbis*: 84; Peter Hvizdak/*The Image Works*: 86

Printed in Malaysia
1 3 5 6 4 2

Contents

Introduction

LIKE ANY OTHER TRAGEDY, the Triangle Shirtwaist Factory fire of March 25, 1911, created undeniable facts and truths. There was no doubt that the death toll of 146 men and women and the gruesome horror of imagining trapped workers jumping out of factory windows and leaping down elevator shafts to save their lives stunned and saddened many. The blaze occurred at a time in the country's history when immigration and industry were booming, and U.S. progress was inarguably pockmarked by the existence of sweatshops and industries with frequently dangerous and dismal labor conditions. Workers at Triangle and other factories across the nation had taken the initial steps to rally for more rights, but yet another unmistakable reality was that their battle would be a long and hard one.

People from congressmen to captains of industry were often unaware of the drudgery that ordinary laborers faced and the life-threatening risks they regularly took merely to earn a week's wages. Meanwhile, business owners had a vested interest in protecting their levels of productivity, though this motivating force sometimes came at the expense of their employees.

With all these indisputable facts about the era in which the Triangle inferno erupted, there nonetheless remain countless questions and the more blurry issues of social conscience versus economic considerations. When 146 lives were lost on March 25, 1911, there was an immediate desire to cast blame. Were New York building inspectors responsible, or did the fault lie with Triangle's owners for operating in violation of fire safety statutes by locking exit doors? Was it possible that the laborers themselves should be held accountable for panicking in the middle of the crisis? Could the finger even be pointed at society as a whole for condoning the existence of sweatshops by turning a blind eye to the plight of the working class?

Similar dilemmas and seemingly unanswerable questions are present nearly one hundred years later, both about the Triangle blaze and the modern sweatshops that continue to exist across the globe. What, if anything, have twenty-first-century citizens learned from the disaster of March 25, 1911, and how have they applied these lessons to current times? What strides did labor groups, business leaders, and heads of state make to rectify working conditions in the early 1900s, and how are these organizations and individuals furthering a legacy of labor rights almost a century after the inferno?

Even with the varying perspectives of differing social factions and players, it is critical to reach common goals and understandings to prevent similar tragedies. Put another way, it is essential to evaluate the historical events surrounding the Triangle Shirtwaist Factory fire, to address the viewpoints of all those affected and involved, and to use this knowledge to ensure that the 146 victims did not die in vain.

One

Industry and Immigration

THE LATE-AFTERNOON HOURS OF MARCH 25, 1911, marked the end of yet another exhausting Saturday for Sylvia Riegler. Like the other 499 garment laborers at the Triangle Shirtwaist Factory on the corner of Greene Street and Washington Place in New York City, she accepted her toil. It was not unusual to be expected to spend anywhere from eight to twelve hours a day at the factory, six days a week.

Yet the events that transpired starting at about 4:45 PM would render the date more unforgettable than Riegler could ever have imagined. A blaze that ripped through the factory that evening would leave a horrific mark on history and countless lives, with 146 workers perishing amid the flames that erupted in the ill-fated sweatshop. Just as important, however, the fire would become a catalyst for national grief, public outrage, and eventually efforts to improve working conditions and safety standards for laborers. But Riegler had no way of foreseeing the future that Saturday in March, and her recollections later served as a grim reminder of an episode the world could not afford to blot from its conscience.

At the Triangle Shirtwaist Factory, garment workers constructed women's blouses, much like those seen here. A horrific fire tore through the factory on the evening of March 25, 1911, killing many of its employees.

I saw men pouring water on the fire at the cutting tables. The wicker baskets where the lace runners worked were beginning to burn. I was scared. [My friend] Rose was pulling me and screaming. Suddenly, I felt I was going in the wrong direction. I broke loose. I couldn't go with her to the windows .... I turned back into the shop. Rose Feibush, my beautiful, dear friend, jumped from a window. .... I don't remember how I got down. I was cold and wet and hysterical. I was screaming all the time. When we came to the bottom, the firemen wouldn't let us out. The bodies were falling all around. They were afraid we would be killed by the falling bodies. I stood there screaming.

Grim Impacts of the Industrial Revolution

Riegler and the majority of the other female garment laborers undoubtedly aspired to do more than stitch women's blouses in the cramped quarters on the eighth and ninth floors of the Triangle Shirtwaist Factory. Yet as recent European immigrants with little money, times were tough enough for them without being particular about employment. Riegler and her coworkers had few options in an early-twentieth-century world that was dominated by industry and riddled with gender discrimination.

The late 1800s and early 1900s marked an era of advancement known as the Industrial Revolution. Innovators seemed to be constantly developing new technology and processes that impacted everything from agriculture to transportation.

Manufacturers in western Europe and the United States built towering factories that mass-produced items at a rapid—and highly profitable—rate.

But while these centers of industry relied more and more on machinery, the machines were impossible to run without multitudes of human laborers. Business owners depended on workers to stand in assembly lines, to throw switches, and to turn gears. In addition, several jobs still involved tasks, such as stitching and cutting, that were more cost-efficient for employers if they were performed by hand. Captains of industry therefore relied on a combination of machinery and human energy to produce the most output at the lowest possible cost.

Conditions in garment factories were merely one example of the work environment that embodied these ideals. New York producers had historically been leaders in supplying the country's demand for ready-made clothes. In the early 1800s plantation owners purchased garments from tailors in this area in an attempt to reduce the time slaves spent piecing together their own clothing. By the mid-1850s New York industrialists eagerly incorporated sewing machines into their manufacturing operations. The next several decades saw local garment companies churning out everything from Civil War military uniforms to the latest styles in women's blouses.

It was not long before New York's Garment District, as it became known by the early 1900s, was filled with garment factories that covered about 1 square mile in midtown Manhattan. Yet the excitement surrounding technological innovations and the enthusiasm of the Industrial Revolution's inventors and entrepreneurs masked darker truths that had taken root inside the factories. These manufacturing centers, which were commonly referred to as sweatshops, fueled garment production at painstaking and sometimes even deadly costs.

It was not uncommon for hundreds of workers to be crammed into tight and unsanitary quarters. Depending on the nature of their particular task, they often labored twelve to thirteen hours a day, six days a week. There was little chance to get outside, to break for meals, to stretch their muscles, or to converse among themselves.

Social reformer Wirt Sikes noted the toll such strenuous labor took on women workers in a factory he toured in the late 1800s.

> There is no attempt at ventilation. The room
> is crowded with girls and women, most of
> whom are pale . . . and are being robbed
> of life slowly and surely. The rose which
> should bloom in their cheeks has vanished
> long ago. The sparkle has gone out of their
> eyes. They bend over their work with aching
> backs and throbbing brows; sharp pains
> dart through their eyeballs; they breathe
> an atmosphere of death.

But the nature of sweatshop workers' toil was not the only horrific aspect of their employment. Conditions within the factories themselves were astoundingly unsafe and unclean. So-called sweatshops could not have been more appropriately named, as laborers unsurprisingly perspired amid the stuffy, stale air that was made worse by the miserable heat.

Many factories did not boast adequate ventilation, and furnaces burned nonstop to power much of the machinery. In addition, fire hazards were amazingly common, despite the fact that a great percentage of them were easy to remedy.

Besides the cramped working areas, scrap materials were often tossed aside carelessly, littering floor space and feeding the blaze when small fires did erupt. It was also not unheard of for foremen to keep doors locked at their discretion, only unlatching exits to allow laborers in or out at opening and closing time. From the perspective of some business owners and factory supervisors, this was neither cruel nor unsafe. It was simply a precautionary measure that discouraged theft

Scraps of fabric accumulate throughout this garment factory during the course of a standard workday. It was scraps such as these that ignited the blaze at the Triangle Shirtwaist Factory.

and kept employees busy at their stations, instead of encouraging them to sneak on and off factory grounds. The practice also prevented union organizers from interfering with day-to-day operations.

Unfortunately, as the fire at the Triangle Shirtwaist Factory would prove, the decision to keep doors locked set the scene for disaster in the event that a blaze could not be immediately halted. Nor were fires the sole safety hazards that plagued sweatshops. Germs spread easily if a single worker simply coughed in the stagnant, overheated air. As if the risk for transmitting disease and contagion in such circumstances was not already great enough, the overcrowded, messy interiors also attracted rats and similar vermin.

Besides, even the healthiest, strongest laborers were at risk of being injured as they operated factory machinery. During that era in American history, mechanical inspections were far from routine, and not all workers were properly trained to use equipment that could sever a limb or scald skin if not handled with great precision. Yet for all the risks they took, sweatshop employees frequently earned only a few dollars a week—compensation that was accurately termed "starvation wages." Given that such individuals endlessly toiled in the shadow of the Industrial Revolution but still barely pocketed enough money to feed and clothe their families, what prompted them to endure the suffering of sweatshops?

Limited Opportunities

The laborers who braved factory work during the early 1900s in New York were frequently men and women who had recently crossed the Atlantic Ocean with dreams of building better lives on American shores. Heralding from

Unconscionable Wages?

Did factory and business owners have crises of conscience when it came to paying their workers starvation wages? Not necessarily, as company heads often were not even aware of what their employees were earning. As with the Triangle Shirtwaist Factory, owners would frequently hire machine operators or subcontractors who would in turn recruit their own teams of laborers. The subcontractors then compensated those workers as they saw fit.

"The girls never knew," said Joseph Fletcher, an assistant cashier at Triangle. "For them, there was no fixed rate. They got whatever the contractor wanted to pay as a start." As far as Triangle's owners were concerned, their payroll reflected the sums they doled out to machine operators, not to the hundreds of individual employees who, in reality, were responsible for production.

such countries as Italy, England, Ireland, Germany, and Russia, they were generally poor, often spoke broken English, and consistently faced discrimination, misunderstanding, and limited opportunities to accomplish what they intended in the United States.

Nonetheless, between 1870 and 1900, almost 12 million immigrants flooded into America from other nations. For more than 70 percent of them, New York City was their point of entrance. Dubbed the Golden Door due to its major role as a center of immigration, the city was ironically anything but golden for its newest arrivals.

Many were forced to live in tenement apartment buildings on Manhattan's Lower East Side. These dwellings were overcrowded and frequently lacked basic amenities, such as indoor plumbing and electricity. Up to seven people sometimes shared a three-room apartment that included a kitchen, a living room, and a single bedroom. One of the sole advantages of living in the cramped tenements was the comparatively cheap rent, which was a necessity for immigrants struggling to enter America's labor force.

The average immigrant had to adapt to new surroundings, a new language, and intermingled suspicion and resentment from U.S. citizens who perceived foreigners as competition in the job market and an unwanted ethnic element in their neighborhoods. Many immigrants had entire families to support and were desperate for employment. Despite the low pay, dangers, and discomforts, factory positions were therefore coveted and regarded as opportunities for those who otherwise lacked career potential—especially immigrant women and children.

In 1910 this two-room apartment on the Lower East Side of Manhattan was the home of an immigrant family of ten.

Those female laborers seeking rights could turn to the International Ladies' Garment Workers' Union (ILGWU). The union was formed in 1900 and was one of the first of its kind to be comprised of mainly women. Yet the ILGWU suffered from internal disagreements on a variety of issues, one of which centered on the complaint that union leaders were primarily interested in protecting the rights of only skilled garment workers. A great number of female

The Realities of a Man's World

Even women who had been U.S. citizens since birth found themselves hard-pressed to secure equal or fair standing in the man's world that defined early-twentieth-century America. Female employees working in industrial settings were paid significantly less than their male counterparts, yet fighting the times was often a fruitless effort and one that was likely to put a worker's job at risk. Ladies who had been fortunate enough to receive some formal schooling could obtain work as teachers or nurses, but most were deemed lucky if they married successful gentlemen who could provide for large families. Women were not formally granted the right to vote until the passage of the Nineteenth Amendment in 1920. Consequently, they had limited say in political efforts that potentially would have expanded the government's role in improving and regulating working conditions.

laborers had no prior experience toiling in a factory and were primarily accustomed to sewing in the context of mending family clothes. However, when they had mouths to feed and rent to pay, how could they possibly turn down a factory job simply because the ILGWU could not guarantee their safety or comfort?

Such women realized that there was intense competition for factory positions, including those that involved sweatshop labor. A laborer who arrived late, left early, or did not show up due to illness or any other circumstance could be easily replaced, regardless of how legitimate or reasonable her excuse. Anyone with the notion of stirring up trouble over issues such as fire hazards or gender discrimination had to be prepared to lose her job in exchange for voicing her opinion. Few factory laborers, however, had the financial luxury of allowing their outspokenness to override their role as breadwinners.

Lithuanian immigrant Pauline Newman worked at the Triangle Shirtwaist Factory as a teenager in the early 1900s. She explained in a letter to friends why she and many of her fellow laborers accepted the indignities of their jobs.

> We knew that individual protest amounted
> to the loss of one's job. No one in those days
> could afford the luxory [*sic*] of changing
> jobs—there was no unemployment
> insurance . . . another job [would] not be
> better than the one we had. Therefore, we
> were, due to our ignorance and poverty,
> helpless against the power of the exploiters.

At the same time, though conditions in sweatshops were hellish, factory owners could not always be characterized as demonic in their treatment of women or of workers in general. For the most part, business proprietors were not deliberately cruel in setting their policies or wage rates. Their role, as they saw it, was to turn a profit by having the lowest manufacturing and employment costs. In a country and society in which women were paid less and had fewer rights than men, factory owners were merely applying the same standards held by everyone, from U.S. politicians to average husbands.

As for failing to provide a safe, sanitary, and comfortable work environment, these proprietors were again not alone. Labor unions and government regulators have since inarguably improved conditions in many factory settings, but this improvement was not a priority for entrepreneurs and businessmen in the early 1900s. The Industrial Revolution was about new machinery and maximal production. Immigrants were in dire need of jobs, and factory owners could not operate without workers.

As much as proprietors may have fallen short in offering employees a safe, healthy way to earn wages, they nonetheless saw themselves as giving the working class an opportunity to earn an honest living. These men focused on the present and near future — sales and products and dollars and cents that played an immediate role in their lives and, inevitably, the lives of their workers. If requiring extended hours or locking fire exits increased productivity and cut down on theft, then ultimately everyone stood to benefit. At the same time, added safety precautions such as extra fire escapes and signage that would have instructed workers as to proper evacuation routes in their primary languages were regarded as extra and unnecessary costs. Anything that detracted from the owner's pocketbooks inevitably also affected employees' salaries, as well. Thus, both manufacturers and the men and women on their payroll had to choose between steady jobs and basic safety.

Sadly, even if conditions in sweatshops were not unique in this era or if immigration and the Industrial Revolution set the stage for output being prioritized over workers' rights, tragedy remained inevitable. Riegler and other laborers at the Triangle Shirtwaist Factory bore witness to that fact on March 25, 1911, a date that would capture the attention of everyone from the wealthiest manufacturers to the humblest immigrants.

Two

The Blaze

THOUGH THE EVENTS OF 1911 WOULD FOREVER distinguish the Triangle Shirtwaist Factory from other early-twentieth-century sweatshops, the company had already fallen under scrutiny for its treatment of laborers. Owners and in-laws Max Blanck and Isaac Harris opened the factory on the ninth floor of the Asch Building, located at 23-29 Washington Place (or 245 Greene Street) in New York City in 1902. They also occupied the eighth and tenth floors by 1908 and fast became known as the Shirtwaist Kings, due to their successful and steady production of button-front women's blouses called shirtwaists.

Blanck and Harris employed five hundred laborers, the majority of whom were young female immigrants from what was then Russia. A small percentage heralded from Italy and Germany. Many of these women were stationed on the ninth floor, which was a cramped and extremely busy hub of activity that housed approximately half of the factory's workforce. It was there that employees made various parts of the shirtwaists, including sleeves, cuffs, and torsos, amid the constant whir of 240 sewing machines. The women sat for seemingly endless stretches at eight 75-foot-long tables

The Success of the Shirtwaist Kings

Exactly how well did their New York City sweatshop serve the Shirtwaist Kings? Though Blanck and Harris owned factories in both New York City and Philadelphia, Pennsylvania, the Asch Building was the site of their general office and a major production center. There were days when more than two thousand garments were created within its walls. The shirtwaists were later sold in batches of twelve at wholesale prices that averaged about $16.50 to $18. As a result, by 1908, Blanck and Harris headed a million-dollar business.

and placed finished garment pieces in troughs throughout the room.

Scraps littered the already cluttered and nearly impassable walkways. A cloakroom, clothes closet, and toilet room also occupied the ninth floor. Despite the room being excessively overcrowded, the workers were required to move quickly and efficiently. Their wages, which were about $6 a week, could be docked if they produced flawed materials, and their jobs could be terminated if they failed to maintain a rapid pace.

One floor below, some women operated sewing machines at five long tables, while others added lace and snipped loose threads at finishing stations. Superior in employment status to the female laborers were the male garment cutters, who cut fabric and commanded higher wages. Altogether, about two hundred workers were situated on the eighth floor. The tenth floor, on the other hand, primarily housed the company offices and areas designated for pressing, packing, and shipping the shirtwaists. The remainder of the factory's approximately five hundred employees spent time on this level of the Asch Building.

Smoking was prohibited on factory grounds, but this directive was frequently ignored, especially by several of the male garment cutters. Violators of the rule had little regard for the fact that sparks from a lit cigarette could ignite a blaze that would race through the littered aisles, where fabric would assuredly act as fodder. This particular hazard, however, was but one item on a long list of safety and health offenses that workers were forced to tolerate.

Yet not every employee at the Triangle Shirtwaist Factory was content to remain completely silent. In November

1909 about four hundred female laborers took part in a spontaneous walkout to protest the poor working conditions and abysmal wages. Between that month and the following February, approximately 20,000 New Yorkers in the shirt-waist trade joined in a strike that later became known as the Uprising of 20,000. The ILGWU and the Women's Trade Union League (WTUL) pushed for stricter safety measures,

In winter 1909 these two garment workers took part in a walkout protesting low wages and poor working conditions.

shorter workweeks, better pay, and factory owners' recognition of and cooperation with unions.

When the strike ended in February, many businessmen in the garment industry had capitulated to several of the laborers' demands, but the Shirtwaist Kings proved less relenting. They insisted on a minimum of a fifty-nine-hour workweek, refused to bend on safety issues such as keeping doors unlocked and maintaining functional fire escapes, and were less than receptive to establishing a relationship with labor unions.

Though the strike proved that factory workers could indeed unite against exploitation, the year ahead saw little changed for the women at the Triangle Shirtwaist Factory. Laborers' anxieties undoubtedly heightened when they heard of a fire at a garment factory in Hackensack, New Jersey, in late 1910 that resulted in the deaths of twenty-five female employees. Edward Croker, New York City's fire chief, even ominously warned that his jurisdiction was home to factories that could serve as the setting for comparable tragedies. By 1911 his speculation would become a terrible truth.

Disaster on the Eighth and Tenth Floors

Shreds of cotton garments and tissue paper used for pattern making cluttered the floor and overwhelmed the Triangle Shirtwaist Factory's scrap bins as quitting time, which was about 4:45 PM, approached on March 25. As usual, the seamstresses prepared to have their pocketbooks checked by factory watchmen for any sign of thievery before they were permitted to leave. Other weary workers such as garment cutter Joseph Granick got ready to end another day of drudgery that was — thus far — similar to any other day at the Triangle Shirtwaist Factory. Granick later recalled, however, the first signs that the evening would be dangerously distinct as he made his way to the Greene Street exit on the eighth floor and encountered Eva Harris, the sister of one of the owners.

"Eva Harris said she smelled something burning," recollected Granick. "I looked to the cutting tables. At the second table, through the slot under the top, I saw the red flames." To this day, the exact source of the fire remains unverified. Though a burning cigarette butt is the likely culprit, an overheated machine engine or faulty electrical wiring is also a possibility. Regardless of what started the blaze, though, there is no doubt that it was steadily fed by garment scraps and other litter and could not be easily extinguished.

Cutter Max Rothen described the ferocity with which the fire spread despite workers' efforts to quell it with buckets of water. "Light scraps of burning fabric began to fly around the room. They came down on the other tables, and they fell on the machines."

Samuel Bernstein, the factory manager and a relative of both owners, ordered that the hoses hanging in a nearby stairwell be brought to the eighth floor immediately. Unfortunately, insufficient water pressure rendered the hoses useless. It was time to focus on evacuating the building rather than eradicating the fire.

By 4:45 PM, the first telegraph signal had been sent from Box 289, the factory's fire alarm box, to notify Fire Department Central of the blaze. Records show workers placed two telephone calls to the fire station approximately half a minute later. Meanwhile, a bookkeeper named Dinah Lipschitz on the eighth floor phoned upstairs to make staff on the factory's two uppermost levels aware of the inferno. She successfully contacted the tenth floor, where owners Blanck and Harris were situated, but her attempts to reach the ninth floor proved problematic. Any calls between the eighth and ninth floors had to be directed by a switchboard operator on the tenth floor, and she was not present at her station.

As Lipschitz and Bernstein realized with mounting terror that the workers on the most crowded level of the factory were likely ignorant of the emergency, hysteria erupted on the eighth floor. Several of the women were darting to the cloakroom in an attempt to salvage the new spring coats and hats they had recently used their hard-earned money to purchase. Bernstein ordered them to abandon the clothes and leave the building, but following his instructions was not as simple as it seemed.

The eighth-floor Greene Street exit was inaccessible due to flames and smoke, and the Washington Place exit remained locked. What had been done as a precautionary measure to prevent theft had become a threat to workers' survival. Luckily, the machinist Louis Brown had a key, but he had to shove through throngs of frenzied young women to make his way to the door.

When Brown finally managed to push open the Washington Place exit—which, like the majority of doors in the factory, only opened inward—many of the panicked laborers tumbled down the spiral staircase, some fainting in the process.

A similar scenario was simultaneously occurring on the outside fire escape, as Brown had also opened a window that allowed workers access to the single set of rickety, slatted stairs that ran along the building's northern facade. The girls who scrambled to leave the factory via this route found themselves tripping, falling, and often crawling back in through broken windows on lower levels in an attempt to locate a safer, more expedient way down.

The only other way off the eighth floor was via two passenger elevators on the west side of the building, but clamor and confusion reigned there, as well. Elevator operators had already begun responding to calls from the tenth floor and—to the horror of employees on the eighth level—did not immediately stop as they made their way up.

"I broke the window of the elevator door with my hands," worker Irene Seivos later recollected. "[I] screamed, 'Fire! Fire! Fire!' It was so hot we could scarcely breathe. When the elevator did stop, and the door opened at last, my dress was catching fire." Seivos's account was far from an emotional exaggeration. At 4:46 PM, the firefighters of Company 72 arrived at the Triangle Shirtwaist Factory. As Captain Howard Ruch made his way to the eighth floor, he quickly surveyed the power of the inferno.

"The fire was so intense it was impossible to stand up," Ruch noted. "We lay down on our stomachs to try to make an entrance. The eighth floor was a mass of fire." Though the other two levels of the factory were not yet engulfed, panic escalated throughout the building. On the tenth floor Blanck had been made aware of the blaze and "didn't seem to know which way to turn," according to Edward N. Markowitz, an employee in charge of the shipping room. Complicating an already dire situation for Blanck was the fact that the family nursemaid had brought his twelve- and five-year-old daughters to meet him at the factory that day.

This dramatic photo of the charred remains of the Triangle Shirtwaist Factory was taken after the flames were extinguished.

Initially, co-owner Harris directed the packed eleva-tors that transported throngs of screaming workers from the tenth floor downward. Harris instructed the operators to return immediately after dispatching the first load of employees on the ground level. Meanwhile, workers on the two floors below watched helplessly as the elevators, which were already filled to capacity, shuttled past them without halting.

Even for employees on the tenth level, however, the elevators offered little reassurance. They were painstakingly slow in comparison to the blaze that was spreading from the eighth floor with alarming speed. Harris, Blanck, and their companions soon comprehended that their sole hope of salvation was the roof. Taking the Greene Street stairs, they headed upward, most choking from the smoke and some scorched by the flames.

Once atop the Asch Building, evacuees turned to face opposite edifices on Greene Street and Washington Place. They could potentially leap to these nearby rooftops—though they towered 13 to 15 feet taller than the Asch Building itself—by climbing onto the building extensions that stretched over the factory's elevator shafts. Occupants of the adjacent New York University–American Book Company Building on Greene Street aided the stranded escapees in their endeavors.

A law professor and his students had fortuitously heard the roar of the fire engines and peered out the window to see the chaos that was erupting next door. Spotting the victims on top of the Asch Building, they raced to their own rooftop and grabbed ladders that painters had set aside there. They then extended the ladders to the dozens of people who subsequently climbed—or were carried—to the safety of the New York University–American Book Company Building.

In the end, only one of the approximately seventy men and women working on the factory's tenth floor perished that day. Most eighth-floor occupants, despite their early terror at facing doors that initially were locked and elevators that refused to stop, managed to scramble down stairwells and the rickety fire escape. Who, then, comprised the majority of the 146 casualties who fell prey to the smoke and flames that evening?

Jump or Burn

"We didn't have a chance," recalled Rose Glantz, a worker on the ninth floor of the Triangle Shirtwaist Factory. "The people on the eighth floor must have seen the fire start and grow. The people on the tenth floor got the warning over the telephone. But with us on the ninth, all of a sudden the fire was all around. The flames were coming in through many of the windows." As Glantz correctly assessed, ninth-floor employees had been left at several disastrous disadvantages.

In addition to the factors Glantz noted, the ninth level was by far the most crowded, with the greatest percentage of workers and row upon row of sewing machines that all stitched highly flammable cotton cloth. By the time the first few ninth-floor laborers took the Greene Street stairs and saw that the eighth floor was in flames, it was already too late for several of their coworkers still one story above. Ninth-floor laborers in the Greene Street stairwell were herded downstairs by firefighters before they had a chance to run back and warn their coworkers, many of whom were also family members and cherished friends.

Unaware of the blaze on the floor beneath them, most of the ninth-floor employees had not even reached either of the exits and were instead clustered around the cloakroom or inside the coat closet. They were chatting, singing, and eagerly anticipating the evening ahead and the much-treasured day of rest that would follow. The excited clamor of female voices was abruptly replaced, however, by the sound of glass shattering as the heat of the inferno caused ninth-floor windows to break.

Once the workers realized what was happening, some dashed to the Washington Place exit, only to find it locked, as had initially been the case with the Washington Place door on the eighth floor. Unfortunately, this time, there was no one with a key to come to the rescue—just a group of horrified women banging their fists in vain.

A handful of employees were lucky enough to access the Greene Street stairwell before it was completely engulfed in flames, but it was only a matter of minutes before that exit became impassable. Other laborers raced for the poorly constructed fire escape, which was clogged with smoke and all but collapsing under the weight of desperate evacuees who shoved one another as they blindly stumbled downward. Button puncher Abe Gordon was the final worker to safely utilize the fire escape that day. He observed the following as he climbed back into the building through a sixth-story window: "I stepped back into the building. I still had one foot on the fire escape when I heard a loud noise and looked back up. The people were falling all around me, screaming all around me. The fire escape was collapsing."

For those who remained trapped on the ninth floor, passenger elevator operators Gaspar Mortillalo and Joseph Zito offered the only opportunity for rescue. After picking

The blazing inferno of the Triangle Shirtwaist Factory caused this fire escape ladder to twist and collapse under the intense heat of the flames and the weight of those trying to escape down its steps. Many workers dropped to their deaths.

up passengers on the tenth floor, the men stopped at the two levels below, with Zito estimating that he made one trip to the eighth floor and four or five to the ninth. Ultimately, however, the elevators could not make any additional trips. The heat had warped the tracks in Mortillalo's elevator shaft, and a more morbid obstacle blocked Zito's path. Forced to decide between burning and plummeting nine stories to the ground, some women leapt into the elevator shaft and onto the top of Zito's car. A few others grasped the cables and attempted to slide down that way. A fortunate handful survived such daring moves; those who did not or who lost consciousness weighed down the elevator and crushed its roof.

As to the rest of the ninth-floor occupants, onlookers and passersby got a terrifyingly unforgettable glimpse of what became of victims who were not consumed by the flames. Journalist Charles Willis Thompson described the sight of bodies falling as garment laborers flung themselves from windows and plunged downward. "It conveys no picture to the imagination to say that the fire was 100 feet above the street: Figures don't make pictures," Thompson observed. "But when you stand on the street and almost topple over backward craning your neck to see a place away up in the sky and realize the way those bodies came hurtling down over the inconceivable distance, it seems more as if it were 100 miles."

Though rescue workers tried to break the workers' fall with a net, the velocity with which the women sped toward the pavement was too great; in some cases, they slammed into already horrified bystanders. Firefighters were forced

Recollections of a Triangle Elevator Operator

It was during his stops on the ninth floor that Zito witnessed a dark foreshadowing of the impossible choice that workers then faced—jump or burn. "When I first opened the elevator door on the ninth floor," he later remembered, "all I could see was a crowd of girls and men with great flames and smoke right behind them. When I came to the floor the third time, the girls were standing on the window sills with the fire all around them."

to maneuver between corpses and injured victims as they struggled to position their ladders, which stretched no farther than the seventh floor of the Asch Building. In the end they managed to extinguish the blaze about eighteen minutes after the moment of their arrival. Survivors were transported hurriedly to area hospitals, but the magnitude

Firefighters attempt to douse the flames of the burning Asch Building.

of the devastation was apparent to everyone, from reporters to police to average citizens, even after the last spark had ceased to burn.

Fifty-four workers had leapt to their deaths that day; another ninety-two had succumbed to the smoke and fire. Those who escaped with their lives were in shock, had been subdued by their injuries, or were at the very least trying to comprehend what had just occurred. Many were desperately searching for loved ones with whom they had once toiled inside the Triangle Shirtwaist Factory. There were some happy reunions outside the Asch Building and in local hospitals, but there were just as many painful real-izations and moments of uncertainty.

The front page of the March 26, 1911, *Brooklyn Daily Eagle* describes the events of the Triangle Shirtwaist Factory fire, which occurred the day before.

Yet one thing was inarguably clear — as word of the disaster spread almost as rapidly as the blaze itself had, someone would have to account for the tremendous and seemingly senseless loss of life. Thompson summed up the sentiments of the multitude when he pointedly remarked, "The first impression when I got down there and looked at the building where the Triangle Waist Company had burned up girls and men was that I would like to hold the rope if there was any general movement to hang Blanck and Harris."

Three

Aftermath of the Inferno

THE DAYS IMMEDIATELY FOLLOWING THE FIRE stirred up powerful emotions. They were only made more intense by the grim task of removing victims' charred remains from the building for identification. As news of the blaze rippled across the country and throughout the city from hospitals and newspaper offices to the tenement houses, families and friends flocked to the Bellevue Morgue on Twenty-Sixth Street and a makeshift morgue on the Twenty-Sixth Street Pier.

Throngs of New Yorkers, consisting of everyone from mourners to concerned relatives to curious onlookers, crowded around the Asch Building days after the last flame had been extinguished. Police attempted to hold back the masses, though they were frequently overwhelmed by the daunting work of combing through the charred interior of the factory to hunt for corpses that were often burned beyond recognition. In such cases, the coroner and next of kin relied heavily on jewelry or trinkets to link human remains to the names of men and women who never returned from work on March 25. It took a week to identify the majority of the dead.

Amid all the grief, however, was a clearly discernible public outcry against such a massive waste of human life.

Yet who was the appropriate target of the mounting hostilities in New York's streets and across the globe? On March 27, a newspaper called the *New York Evening Journal* ran a political cartoon on its front page that featured a picture of a gallows and the pointed caption, "This ought to fit somebody; who is he?" The message could not have more appropriately expressed the dilemma that wracked

Crowds at the Twenty-Sixth Street Pier wait to enter the morgue to identify the bodies of the victims of the Triangle Shirtwaist Factory fire.

Mourners in an Unfamiliar Land

Relatives of the victims of the blaze lost far more than loved ones; they were also suddenly deprived of family breadwinners. Luckily, everyone from the WTUL to the Red Cross to the mayor of New York City took up contributions for the bereaved. They also saw to the needs of dependents who had been orphaned and consequently needed to be returned to the care of relations overseas. As representatives of the ILGWU explained to the public in their appeal for donations, "Everyone knows that the victims of this terrible catastrophe were poor working people whose families are either left destitute or can ill afford the cost of sickness or death. The sole support of the family in many cases has been swept away."

bereaved families, political officials, and the heads of the Triangle Shirtwaist Factory. The fury and frustration that resulted from the fire were undeniable, but finding the right person—or people—to blame for the bloodshed was far less clear-cut.

Unions such as the ILGWU organized meetings and protests, and even gatherings at churches and synagogues

In 1911 labor union members protest and mourn the loss of their fellow garment workers.

reflected an urgent and passionate push to hold the responsible parties accountable. "One of the hard facts that will confront these bereaved," reflected Reverend Doctor Charles L. Slattery at Grace Church on Broadway and Eleventh Street shortly after the blaze, "is that it will probably be explained that the death of their loved ones was needless. It will perhaps be discovered that someone was too eager to make money out of human energy to provide the proper safeguards and protection."

The Dilemma of Assigning Blame

The coroner's office, the district attorney, fire commissioner Rhinelander Waldo, and acting building department superintendent Albert Ludwig hurriedly orchestrated investigations that focused on the Asch Building. Politicians and city officials all echoed each other's sentiments of being appalled at recent events, but it came as no great surprise that not a single one appeared ready to accept or acknowledge any blame. As personal responsibility was handed from one public figure to another in newspaper stories and public declarations, discussion shifted to the past—specifically, ten years prior, when construction was completed on the Asch Building in January 1901.

The owner, Joseph J. Asch, ultimately claimed that, at that time, architects had assured him that his building was fireproof and met the specifications required by the building code. A decade later, however, closer examination revealed that what was deemed acceptable in 1901 proved problematic in the years that followed. For starters, the Asch Building technically should have had three staircases because of its square footage per floor, but it had only two. Yet its architects had objected to this requirement because they feared it would negatively affect the exterior appearance. They consequently convinced the Buildings Department that the fire escape essentially constituted the third stairway.

In regard to the poor construction of the fire escape itself, which was even noted by a building inspector during construction, no law required fire escapes, fire drills, or sprinkler systems. It was therefore impractical to suggest that a building owner improve or add such structures and practices when they were not mandated in the first place. True, the New York State Labor Law insisted that the doors inside factories "shall be so constructed as to open outwardly . . . and shall not be locked, bolted, or fastened during working hours." More to the point, a 1909 inspection by a fire-prevention expert had been conducted for insurance purposes and had concluded that there were overcrowded working conditions within the top three floors of the Asch Building.

But Asch himself claimed that he had never been approached by the Buildings Department to alter the building in any way. Did blame therefore lie with building inspectors for not having been more vigilant in insisting on changes? For his part, Ludwig stressed that his staff was already overworked and operating with scant resources.

"For us," he explained defensively, "[it is impossible] with our limited number of inspectors, to make regular examinations of the buildings that have once been passed as filling the terms of the law. The best we can do is to look into specific complaints that are brought to us from outside sources."

Looking to New York's Labor Department

Did the New York Labor Department acknowledge any responsibility for the events of March 25, 1911? Though the agency admitted that it had received complaints about the Triangle Shirtwaist Factory, it, too, claimed innocence. "The State Labor Department has no supervision in the matter of fire escapes in Manhattan," insisted former first deputy state labor commissioner W. W. Walling. "At the time of the shirtwaist strike, we investigated strikers' complaints that too many persons were working . . . in the factory of the Triangle Shirtwaist Company. The complaint was unwarranted. Under the law, each worker must have 250 cubic feet of air space, and this the Triangle employees had."

Given the arguments of Ludwig and numerous other city officials, who best fit in the noose depicted in the *New York Evening Journal*? Because so much guilt could be washed away by claims that inspections had been conducted and that building and safety codes had originally been met, government employees could insist that the majority of hazards that *did* exist were typical of the era and were not problems the building owner was required to correct.

Yet the locked door at the Washington Place exit on the ninth floor was damning. There was no question that locked

Inspectors view one of the locked doors at the Triangle Shirtwaist Factory.

doors were specifically prohibited by law during the factory's business hours. The only real question was whether Blanck and Harris were aware of the violation that ultimately played a role in 146 gruesome — and clearly unnecessary — fatalities. By April 11, authorities believed they had sufficient evidence to indict Blanck and Harris on charges of first- and second-degree manslaughter.

In the Hands of the Court

Though the Triangle Shirtwaist Factory owners were indicted in April, jury selection did not get underway until December 1911. Activists, however, put the intervening months to good use. On June 30, New York State created the Factory Investigating Commission (FIC), which evaluated the need for improved laws that could potentially prevent similar fires. It ultimately inspected 1,836 factories and interviewed 222 witnesses before issuing several reports in the years that followed the Triangle fire. Historians credit the commission with ushering in "the golden era in remedial factory legislation," during which New York enacted thirty-six new safety and labor laws.

The ILGWU and other labor groups also continued to meet and were determined that workers' rights must and would be expanded, so that the events of March 25 would never be repeated. The ILGWU and WTUL organizer Rose Schneiderman expressed as much at an April 2 gathering that was intended to memorialize the victims of the fire. "I would be a traitor to these poor burned bodies if I came here to talk good fellowship," said Schneiderman during a speech. She continued,

We have tried you good people of the
public, and we have found you wanting.
The old Inquisition had its rack and its
thumbscrews and its instruments of torture
with iron teeth. We know what these things
are today; the iron teeth are our necessities,
the thumbscrews are the high-powered and
swift machinery close to which we must
work, and the rack is here in the firetrap
structures that will destroy us the minute
they catch on fire.

Similar sentiments resounded in the Criminal Courts
Building in early December, as friends and family members of Triangle victims hounded Blanck and Harris with cries
of "Murderers! Murderers!" when the owners entered and
exited the courtroom. The owners' fate lay in the hands of
twelve jurors, who analyzed the testimony of 155 witnesses over
a period of 18 days. Judge Thomas C. T. Crain presided.
Max D. Steuer served as legal counsel for the defense, and
attorneys Charles Bostwick and J. Robert Rubin prosecuted.

Much to his benefit, Steuer heralded from New York
City's Lower East Side, where many of the laborers
who were called by the prosecution as witnesses lived in
crowded tenement apartments. The defense attorney was
therefore well aware that the majority of factory girls who
took the stand would be awed by their surroundings in the
courtroom and perhaps daunted by their inability to fully
comprehend English. Intelligent and quick-witted, Steuer
was detailed and prodding in his interrogations of men and

women whom he believed were perhaps perjuring themselves out of understandable anger and resentment at the loss of their loved ones.

Steuer's primary argument was that the Washington Place door on the ninth floor was actually unlocked but was not a practical means of escape because fire had consumed the nearby stairwell. He questioned why, if workers were indeed accustomed to that exit being locked, they had flooded to it when they learned of the blaze. Why had they not instead rushed for the Greene Street stairs? While Steuer did not blame the victims for their fate in an outright fashion, he suggested that laborers had panicked and had not clearly reasoned the best evacuation route when they learned of the fire.

The prosecution addressed Steuer's speculation by insisting that the Washington Place door *had* been locked and that, had it not been, lives would have been saved. They noted how eighth-floor employees had escaped via the stairwell on that side of the building, so the fire had not initially rendered that exit impassable. In addition, the prosecutors insisted that the laborers had not automatically flocked to the Washington Place door. Several, they argued, had evacuated through the Greene Street exit. They emphasized that others were not able to because the fire had, in fact, spread through that stairwell first.

To drive their point home, Bostwick and Rubin even presented a lock that they claimed two workmen had found amid the debris and rubble on the ninth floor following the inferno. Steuer quickly countered by casting doubts as to the authenticity of the object, especially as the fire department had carefully searched the Asch Building for such a lock immediately after the disaster and had come up empty-handed. The prosecution's lock, Steuer shrewdly observed, was miraculously discovered on April 10, the day before Blanck and Harris were formally indicted.

Yet Bostwick and Rubin invited experts ranging from engineers to hardware salesmen to prove that their evidence was entirely valid. The question then became whether the ninth-floor Washington Place exit was locked on March 25 and whether Blanck and Harris were aware of the violation. For his part, Steuer called fifty-two witnesses, most of whom either held nonproduction jobs with the Triangle Shirtwaist Factory or had little reason to be at the Asch Building on a daily basis. Factory manager Samuel Bernstein testified that the door was unlocked, but his credibility was called into question, as he was related to the owners through marriage. Others who took the stand for the defense voiced the same assertion but invited similar suspicions about how much they valued facts and truth above their employment status.

Blanck and Harris also testified, the latter explaining the legitimacy of using locks and the necessity of searching workers for stolen goods at the end of the day. "We once locked up about six girls, and we found . . . so many waists, and we had detectives that went around there, and we . . . found from two dozen to three dozen waists that these girls had taken." Regardless of his and Blanck's presumed fault in the matter, it seemed that neither man was a monster who would have wished death on his laborers. In their minds, they were simply exercising due diligence in protecting their property from repeated incidents of theft.

In the face of the owners' testimony, however, were the impassioned accounts of Triangle employees who argued that the door *was* locked and was ultimately the main factor that resulted in the demise of their coworkers. To their credit, such individuals—who served as the prosecution's main witnesses apart from firefighters and technicians—made up in courage and passion what they lacked in language abilities or courtroom experience. Over and over, they relayed vivid descriptions of victims futilely trying to dash from the flames, and over and over, they repeated the refrains "The door was locked," or "I pushed at the door, and it would not open."

Steuer did his best to discredit the witnesses' statements by asking them to repeat their accounts of March 25, frequently calling attention to even the most minor of inconsistencies. By December 27, the day Crain ordered the jurors to deliberate and to reach a verdict, the words of 155 witnesses were somewhat clouded. Emotions understandably ran high on either side of the case, and attorneys had explanations for why the oppositions' testifiers had valid reasons to exaggerate or to fabricate.

The judge attempted to clarify the role of the jury with the following directive: "You must be satisfied from the evidence . . . not merely that the door was locked—if it was locked—but that it was locked . . . under circumstances bringing knowledge of that fact to these defendants."

Nearly two hours later, Blanck and Harris were found not guilty. As one juror explained,

> I cannot see that anyone was responsible for the disaster. It seems to me to have been an

act of the Almighty. I think that the Blanck
and Harris factory was well managed. I
paid great attention to the witnesses while
they were on the stand. I think the girls who
worked there were not as intelligent as those
in other walks of life and were therefore the
more susceptible to panic.

The mob who listened to the judgment did not agree.
They chased Blanck and Harris to the nearest subway station
as they wailed for their lost loved ones and again accused the
men of murder. Prosecutors attempted to force another trial
in March 1912, but their efforts were fruitless based on the
constitutional provision that prohibits trying someone for
the same crime twice. Meanwhile, the Triangle Shirtwaist
Factory had resumed operations in a building on Sixteenth
Street and Fifth Avenue.

The company name was spotted for the last time in a
New York City directory in 1918, and Blanck and Harris
dissolved their partnership in 1920. Prior to that point, the
business was intermittently cited for further violations of
labor laws, but thankfully none resulted in the grievous outcome of the 1911 inferno. In March 1914 Blanck and Harris
settled twenty-three individual civil suits related to the blaze
at seventy-five dollars per life lost. Ultimately, however, such
a price tag did little to compensate family and friends of the
deceased, who had expended time and both monetary and
emotional resources to fight for justice and restore stability
to the existences of the countless children, and relatives who
had been left to cope with the passing of loved ones.

By spring 1914, such individuals were forced to wearily accept the fact that it was time to move on—without many solid assurances that the carnage that occurred three years prior would never be repeated.

"The claimants have been tired out," a periodical called *The World* reported that year. "Their money and their patience have been exhausted. So far as personal guilt is concerned, the men whose methods made everything ready for the tragedy have gone free. So far as financial liability is concerned, the whole affair is in the hands of an insurance company, and stricken families are not well equipped to carry on expensive litigations with corporations." In the middle of such pervasive defeat, was it conceivable that the death and destruction of March 1911 could lead to reforms that would eclipse the pain and ashes?

Four

The Martyrs of Labor Reform

There was a stricken conscience of public guilt, and we all felt that we had been wrong, that something was wrong with that building, which we had accepted or the tragedy never would have happened. Moved by this sense of stricken guilt, we banded ourselves together to find a way by law to prevent this kind of disaster. . . . It was based really upon the experiences that we had in New York State and upon the sacrifices of those [whom] we faithfully remember with affection and respect [and who] died in that terrible fire on March 25, 1911. They did not die in vain, and we will never forget them.

So spoke Frances Perkins, witness to the blaze, workers' advocate, and the U.S. secretary of labor under President Franklin Delano Roosevelt from 1933 to 1945. Perkins, who served as executive secretary of the New York Committee on Safety at the time of the fire, played an important role in aiding the FIC.

A proponent of women's rights, Frances Perkins witnessed the Triangle fire and garment workers leaping to their death.

Like so many other U.S. citizens invested in improving labor rights, Perkins was dedicated to ensuring that the 146 fatalities of 1911 inspired positive and immediate change. This goal was partially realized in October 1911 with the passage of the Sullivan-Hoey Law, which led to the establishment of the New York Bureau of Fire Prevention. In addition to bolstering safety precautions and regulations, the new legislation amplified the responsibilities and jurisdiction of the fire commissioner. Immediately following the inferno, members of the city's fire department had irritably emphasized the number of times they had observed the lack of adequate and acceptable fire escapes and the need for drills and placards written in different languages indicating escape routes.

"Those responsible for buildings," noted Fire Chief Croker, "include the Tenement House Department; the Factory Inspection Department; the Building Department; the Health Department; the Department of Water Supply, Gas, and Electricity; and the Police Department to see that the orders of the other five departments are carried out. Yet the Fire Department doesn't have a word to say about fire escapes or fire exits." Thanks to the Sullivan-Hoey Law, Croker and his counterparts finally had the authority to mandate changes within a factory setting in order to avoid disaster, rather than being limited to merely noting obvious hazards.

Investigations, Improvements, and a Golden Era of Labor Reforms

In addition to promoting preventive legislation such as the Sullivan-Hoey Law, many social activists supported the unions.

The WTUL, the ILGWU, the National Consumers League (NCL), and other groups all gathered, rallied, and ultimately won a major victory when the New York State Legislature established the FIC in the summer of 1911. The next four years were filled with detailed inspections of the city's workplaces, with members of the commission scrutinizing potential hazards. State laws enacted as a result of the investigations required everything from improved ventilation to fire alarms, fire drills, and sprinkler systems.

The commission eventually turned its attention to the problems that plagued workers in other industries. Members examined conditions in businesses that involved baking, tobacco, printing, chemicals, and countless other types of manufacturing. They also evaluated factories for far more than fire hazards; men, women, and children often toiled in settings that were overcrowded and unsanitary. These workers labored long hours that tested their physical endurance and rarely provided sufficient compensation to allow them to escape poverty. In essence, there were scores of factories throughout the state that had the potential to serve as the setting of another tragedy.

In 1912 the commission issued a report that unabashedly detailed its findings.

> Many of our industries were found housed in palatial loft buildings, and employ[ed] the most improved machinery and mechanical processes. . . . But at the same time, [such industries] greatly neglect[ed] the care, health and safety of their employees. Our system of industrial production has taken

The FIC investigated child labor and the harsh conditions under which children worked.

gigantic strides in the progressive utilization of natural resources and the exploitation of the inventive genius of the human mind, but has at the same time shown a terrible waste of human resources, of human health, and life. It is because of this neglect of the human

factor that we have found so many
preventable defects in industrial
establishments, such a large number of
workshops with inadequate light and
illumination, with no provision for
ventilation, without proper care
for cleanliness, and without ordinary
indispensable comforts such as washing
facilities, water supply, toilet
accommodations, dressing rooms, etc.

These observations were submitted to New York's legislative bodies on an annual basis, and lawmakers subsequently enacted thirty-six safety statutes that did everything from mandating fire escapes to limiting women's and children's workweeks. Starting in 1914 laborers from these two groups could spend only fifty-four and forty-eight hours per week working in factories, respectively.

The commission's other success was forcing the passage of laws that required business owners to provide basic sanitation and comfort, including functional washrooms and seats that supported employees' backs if they had to labor in a sitting position for several hours. Members also fought for regulations that would support machine guarding, or the installation of barriers and shields that prevented workers' body parts from coming into direct contact with dangerous equipment. All in all, the commission's achievements were remarkable and unmatched for their time. As Perkins proudly assessed, they were what caused the flames of the Triangle Shirtwaist Factory fire to become the "torch that lighted up the industrial scene."

Seeing to the Needs of Working Mothers

Thanks to the FIC, the new state labor codes even addressed how soon female employees could return to their jobs after childbirth. Prior to the commission's efforts, women often resumed their work almost immediately after having their babies, largely because many justifiably worried that their positions would otherwise be filled. In turn, however, they frequently suffered intense physical stress by taking up a rigorous work routine so soon after delivery. Legislation passed in 1912 required that women not return to factories any sooner than four weeks subsequent to childbirth.

Different Perspectives and Continued Progress

Not everyone, however, was delighted by the burst of "illumination" that Perkins perceived. The commission undeniably had the support of several powerful figures, including state legislators Robert Wagner and Al Smith; Samuel Gompers, president of the American Federation of Labor; social activist Perkins; and Governor William Sulzer, who was elected in 1912. Yet business and building owners argued that the commission stirred controversy that stemmed from sensational and exaggerated accounts offered up by investigators who lacked expertise. From a fiscal standpoint, taking precautionary measures such as the installation of sprinkler systems and machine guards was costly.

The businessmen who raised objections to the commission's efforts were, in many cases, far from hard-hearted, penny-pinching, or deliberately cruel. After experiencing decades of little to no regulation by the New York State Labor Department, they were suddenly expected to make scores of expensive renovations that cut into their profits and affected their livelihoods. It was one thing to ensure that doors remained unlocked during working hours, but it was quite another to be forced to install a five thousand dollar sprinkler system. As the *New York Times* reported in May 1914, the commission's enthusiasm inevitably drove several businesses to seek greener pastures in other states, where labor legislation was not yet as stringent.

A startling illustration of the present
mercantile and factory real estate conditions

in New York is found in the district between
Chambers Street and Fourteenth Street on
Broadway. One cannot walk through this
district and [not] observe the 'To Let'
signs . . . to the east and west without
realizing the gravity of the situation.
You can no longer distinguish the real
estate owner by the smile of prosperity
because his property is now a burden and
a liability instead of a comfort and a source
of income. To own a factory building in
New York City is now a calamity.

The businessmen who could attest to this sentiment took
some satisfaction in Governor Sulzer's impeachment in 1913.
Not only had the politician been a strong proponent of the
commission, but his removal from office crippled the Demo-
cratic Party, which was also overwhelmingly supportive of
labor reform. Opponents of the FIC seized the opportunity
to hit back at the commission legislatively by pushing forth
"ripper" bills that focused on the language of the new laws.
For example, they quibbled over how the word *factory* was
defined, which enabled some work environments to be merely
subject to the authority of local police. If a place of business
could not technically be termed a factory, owners were not
subject to the stricter judgment of the labor department.

In the end, though, the vast majority of such bills never
entered state law books. The new governor, Martin H. Glynn,
vetoed all but one. Though certain social activists—and
friends and family members of the victims of the 1911

fire—undoubtedly perceived this outcome as a triumph of good over evil, it was in reality more a sign of the changing times. At long last, the might of the massive manufacturing boom was being overshadowed by the realization that Americans of all classes and backgrounds should not sacrifice basic human rights to industry.

"We have put property rights above life," noted Monsignor William J. White, charities director of the Roman Catholic Diocese of Brooklyn. "The workers have a right to life, and it comes before our right to the ease and luxury that flow to the community through the production of the wage earners."

As the years passed, the reprioritization of these rights that took root in New York spread across the country. The U.S. Department of Labor (DOL), set apart from the U.S. Department of Commerce, was officially established in 1913, and many federal officials began taking a more authoritative stance in pushing for further reforms. Several significant policies were passed in the 1930s, during the era of Roosevelt's New Deal, when the president worked aggressively to help the country recover from the Great Depression. The New Deal featured a series of economic plans, most of which were implemented between 1933 and 1940, that set standards relating to everything from wages to public welfare for average Americans. New Deal legislation aided citizens struggling to overcome the economic chaos of the late 1920s and early 1930s. It also served to enhance federal protection of laborers' rights.

For starters, the National Labor Relations Act of 1935, otherwise known as the Wagner Act, gave workers the right

Divisions of the DOL

The DOL operates through numerous agencies, several of which promote and guarantee health and safety in the workplace. The Occupational and Safety Health Administration (OSHA) is one example, as is the Employment Standards Administration (ESA). Nor does the DOL limit itself to the welfare of workers in factories; for instance, organizations such as the Mine Safety and Health Administration (MSHA) regulate working conditions in the mining industry.

to form unions. In addition, the Fair Labor Standards Act of 1938 set minimum wages and maximum weekly hours, effectively outlawing sweatshop production. The labor movement continued to intensify throughout the 1940s. By the following decade, one out of every three workers was a union member. Meanwhile, the DOL further expanded to bring labor rights under national jurisdiction.

Hundreds of members of the Needle Trades Workers Industrial Union gather in Manhattan in 1933 to protest poor working conditions.

The specific purpose of the DOL was initially described as being "to foster, promote, and develop the welfare of working people, to improve their working conditions, and to advance their opportunities for profitable employment." Nearly a century later, the department reasserts these goals and adds that it is also responsible for "protecting [job seekers', wage earners', and retirees'] retirement and healthcare benefits, helping employers find and retain workers, strengthening free collective bargaining, and tracking changes in employment, prices, and other national economic measurements."

The extensive network of DOL agencies is testimony to how far the United States has come in revamping its policies regarding labor rights, but how far does the country—and the world at large—still have to go? From the moment the FIC convened to evaluate these rights to the second the DOL handed down its most recent labor statistics, the nation has clearly undergone major legislative reforms. Since 1911, officials, social activists, union leaders, and workers themselves have banded together to ensure that not a single life, let alone 146, would be lost in circumstances similar to those at the Triangle Shirtwaist Factory. How, then, are sweatshops still able to exist in the twenty-first century, and how has history managed to tragically repeat itself?

Five

An Ongoing Dilemma

"MORE THAN FIFTY PEOPLE HAVE BEEN KILLED and about 100 injured in a fire at a textile mill in Bangladesh, police say." These were the opening lines of a report issued by the British Broadcasting Corporation (BBC) on February 24, 2006, in the wake of a factory blaze in the southern Asian republic. "[It] has been described by officials as the country's worst ever factory fire. . . . Most of the survivors had to jump from windows, as the only exit from the factory was reportedly locked when the fire broke out late on Thursday."

Almost ninety-five years after the inferno at the Triangle Shirtwaist Factory and six years after the dawn of a new century, the same grim and seemingly preventable tragedy appeared to have played out on another continent. Were the similarities merely a bizarre and unique coincidence, or did world leaders have to concede that not enough had truly changed in workplace safety following the events of 1911?

"U.S. apparel employment peaked in the 1970s and has declined ever since," explains Eric Dirnbach, uniform coordinator for UNITE HERE—a North American union that currently represents 450,000 members in several industries, including garment production. "It is relatively easy to set up an apparel factory almost anywhere, and it is much cheaper to produce [apparel] overseas, with wages that are often less than 10 percent of U.S. wages. So, over the past few decades, we have seen the growth of a globalized apparel industry taking place in more than one hundred countries and involving tens of millions of workers."

"Unfortunately," he continues, "sweatshop conditions are the norm for the industry. The major apparel brands send their work to many contractors in many countries, including China, Bangladesh, Indonesia, and Pakistan, and they have been unwilling or unable to ensure that the working conditions are decent. The contractors are in tremendous competition with each other to offer the lowest prices . . . so they cut their labor costs to the minimum. Workers are the ones who suffer in this system that has one goal—to produce cheap clothing quickly."

A popular misconception is that those who suffer always do so in the far reaches of Asia or South or Central America, in countries that do not fall under the authority of the DOL or American unions. However, sweatshops actually exist within U.S. borders as well. A 1996 report by the DOL estimated that "out of 22,000 U.S. garment shops, at least half were in serious violation of wage and safety laws."

In the majority of these scenarios, the situation does not differ greatly from that at the Triangle Shirtwaist Factory. Many sweatshop laborers are immigrants—some legal and others not—who are desperately hunting for a toehold in an economy where it is easier to obtain employment if you speak the dominant language and have had a formal education.

Garment workers, many of whom are immigrants, prepare garments at a midtown Manhattan factory in 1996.

While labor legislation may have been created and updated since the early 1900s, not all workers are universally aware of its existence or knowledgeable about what channels to pursue if it is violated.

For workers in foreign sweatshops, immigration and language barriers may not be issues, but poverty undeniably is.

The Social Life of a Teenage Sweatshop Laborer

Most U.S. teenagers enjoy socializing with their peers and have ample opportunities to do so both at school and around their neighborhoods. Sadly, socializing is a rarity for teens such as Mejia. "What I really don't like about this job is it makes it difficult to have friends. . . . The supervisor slaps you in the face if she sees you talking. She hasn't slapped me yet, but she hits the girl next to me. . . . I don't have a boyfriend, even though I am fifteen. The [factory] is not a great place to meet them. Most of the men use abusive language. . . . When I was younger, I liked basketball and running around the square and visiting my cousins. Now there is no time. I am tired a lot. I don't play much any more."

Many younger workers turn to sweatshops to avoid working in factories where more stringent enforcement of age restrictions established by labor laws would otherwise prevent them from earning income to assist their families. They endure excessive hours, a lack of space and sanitation, and other indignities because they are in desperate need of money. Yet they pay a high price in exchange for making barely enough money to survive.

"Do you think I would do this if we didn't need the money?" reflected Myra Esperanza Mejia in an interview for Pacific News Service in San Francisco, California, in 1997. Fifteen at the time, Mejia was working in a clothing factory in Guatemala that produced pants and dresses that were later sold in the United States. "I liked school. . . . If I didn't need to work, I would be in school."

Still Imprisoned by Exploitation

Poignant as Mejia's account of working in a sweatshop may be, what is particularly striking are the similarities in conditions between her workplace in 1997 and those in the Triangle Shirtwaist Factory in 1911. As the 2006 blaze in Bangladesh also proved, locked doors and other grave safety hazards are not a thing of the past. Foremen and owners still often bar employees from exiting the premises unsupervised, for reasons ranging from fear of theft to a desire to prevent idleness and to boost production. Mejia explained that she earned sixty to sixty-six dollars a week and would toil through round-the-clock shifts an average of eight to twelve times a month. When she or her coworkers voiced their wish to leave for the day, they were routinely forced to remain at the factory.

Assessing Modern-Day Sweatshops

Mejia's description of everyday life as a sweatshop laborer is disturbing but common. In 1997 the DOL observed that almost 67 percent of garment factories in New York City—the setting of the infamous Triangle fire—did not adhere to federal legislation regulating minimum wages and work hours. Unfortunately, such data is often hard to assess due to several factors. These include laborers' fear of losing their jobs or being reported as illegal immigrants, intimidation by factory foremen and owners, and the limited number of inspectors available to tour factories.

"When the bell finally rings at 6:30 PM, you are ready to go home," she noted, "but it is not always possible. If there is more work, the owners tell you they need people to stay for the night shift. If not enough people say yes, the supervisor sits in front of the doors, and no one can leave. The first time this happened, I said, 'My mother will be worried sick if I don't come home—let me tell her, and I'll come back.' They said, 'No—you won't come back.'"

Such testimony regarding modern-day sweatshops paints a portrait of work environments that generally do not offer adequate ventilation, lighting, emergency exits, and sometimes even running water and toilets. Laborers— the majority of whom are female—are commonly subjected to emotional or physical abuse. Most are painfully aware that they can lose their positions in a heartbeat for reasons ranging from pregnancy to complaining about work conditions to affiliating with unions in any way. Some are children and teenagers, and an overwhelming number are paid less than what is considered the standard minimum wage in their country.

These workers frequently and understandably consider themselves "helpless against the power of the exploiters," just as the immigrant and onetime Triangle employee Pauline Newman did in the early 1900s. But are these modern-day exploiters any more black and white in their villainy than Blanck and Harris, or does responsibility for twenty-first-century sweatshops lie with several culprits and society in general? How much lack of regard for labor rights is due to outright greed, and how much is due to the lack of awareness and global standards?

Again, the Question of Guilt

For anyone who witnessed the events of March 25, 1911, or was even remotely connected with one of the 146 victims, the blaze at the Triangle Shirtwaist Factory seemed like it would be impossible to forget. And, while the aforesaid individuals probably never did erase the memory of the flames from their minds, some experts contend that future generations are not necessarily able to immediately identify with the impact of the tragedy.

This is partly due to the fact that the fight for labor rights gained such incredible momentum in the wake of the fire, and conditions appeared to improve consistently for several decades. Trade unions and government regulation helped to close down countless sweatshops, especially following World War II. Starting in the 1980s and 1990s, however, things began to change for the worse. Communist governments toppled in areas such as Eastern Europe, and free trade was suddenly encouraged between countries that previously had not enjoyed economic relationships. A globalized economy took root, which led American industries to outsource production to other continents.

This move not only provided nations struggling to establish more secure democracies with jobs and financial stimulation, but also helped U.S. manufacturers decrease their costs. A globalized economy does not necessarily come with globalized labor rights, and minimum wage requirements vary per country, as does the strength of enforcement. For example, minimum wage is currently set at the equivalent of $39.79 a month in Pakistan, while it's about $936 a month in the United States. While economic

Factory workers in Laos, Korea, assemble garments to be exported abroad.

standards differ around the world, such vastly incomparable labor costs often make it much cheaper for American businesses to manufacture their wares—including garments and clothing—in other nations.

In addition, each government upholds its own set of labor laws, and enforcement can sometimes prove lax. For newly formed or impoverished countries, this does not consistently relate to greed or corruption. Residents of developing nations are typically in dire need of jobs, and officials who turn a blind eye to the deplorable working conditions that exist in foreign-owned factories ironically ensure that their countries continue to receive foreign money.

Explained a different way, manufacturers naturally focus on how much they need to invest in production and how much profit they will gain in return. If it costs more to maintain a factory in a developing country that insists on higher minimum wages and more stringent inspections, business owners can always opt to operate somewhere else. So government officials sacrifice workers' rights to keep business flowing into their national economies.

This is one of the reasons sweatshops continue to exist within U.S. borders as well. Though economists would never refer to the United States as a developing nation, the government is nonetheless eager to sustain business at home. There are also a limited number of DOL inspectors available to tour U.S. production sites, and a great percentage of companies are therefore only required to self-monitor workplace conditions. Even when the DOL finds a business to be in violation of a labor statute, the fines that big-name corporations face are often negligible.

To further complicate matters both at home and abroad, chief executives and business owners often insist that they have no knowledge of what factory conditions are actually like because they subcontract manufacturing to firms that oversee production. Consequently, the men and women one would readily blame for the existence of sweatshops are not always aware of the number of underage employees at a work site in Guatemala or the lack of ventilation at a warehouse in China.

Television personality Kathie Lee Gifford is a famous example of a businesswoman who made news headlines for her involvement with sweatshops. In 1996 a human rights group called the National Labor Committee (NLC) accused Gifford—the owner of a popular clothing line sold at Wal-Mart stores—of utilizing sweatshop production. In May of that year, a fifteen-year-old Honduran girl named Wendy Diaz traveled to the United States and candidly discussed her experiences working at Global Fashions, the South American factory that produced Gifford's sportswear.

"They'd scream at us," Diaz was quoted as saying in a *New York Times* article. "They'd hit us. They'd throw clothes at us. We were only allowed to go to the bathroom twice a day." The young laborer went on to explain that she worked more than sixty hours a week for a mere thirty-four cents an hour, a routine she had begun two years earlier.

In response to the horrific account, Gifford stated that she had not known how deeply workers suffered to manufacture her product. "The era of the sweatshop should have been buried generations ago," she asserted during a series of public declarations in support of universal labor rights. She insisted that she was not involved with the day-to-day aspects of production, vowed to investigate all her work sites accordingly, and made plans to disassociate herself from subcontractors such as Global Fashions.

Yet for Diaz, the victory was hollow. Though the teenager ultimately quit her job, she realized that many of her fellow laborers did not have that option—and that sweatshops would not close shop simply because a single client took her business elsewhere. What she desired—and what progress in labor reform necessitated—were public and political figures such as Gifford to stay and face the issues that had taken root in the workplace. Otherwise, potentially powerful individuals merely voiced their opposition to sweatshops but essentially did little to throw tangible support behind those employees who lacked any real voice at all. "We'd like [Gifford] to return her work to the factory, but with better conditions," Diaz emphasized. The fifteen-year-old had no interest in casting blame on one specific person for the issue. What Diaz did call for, however, was immediate and lasting change. The days following the fire at the Triangle Shirtwaist Factory provided evidence that change is indeed possible, but what can twenty-first-century citizens do to make it enduring?

Six

Promoting Reform and Remembering History

THE CENTENNIAL OF THE TRIANGLE SHIRTWAIST FACTORY FIRE will take place in 2011. It is frustrating to acknowledge that sweatshops still exist and that labor rights still require enforcing. But people across the world continue to chart the course for positive change, from making simple shopping decisions to implementing major policy developments at corporate and national levels. Nearly one hundred years later, what specifically are people doing to guarantee that sweatshops are stamped out once and for all and that the legacy of the 146 victims of March 25, 1911, lives forever?

For starters, several big-name stores and manufacturers are taking a stand by prioritizing labor rights—and human rights in general—over profit at any cost. Reebok, Sears, the Gap, and Wal-Mart are just a sampling of corporate entities that have made efforts to monitor their production sites or to subcontract only to companies that are known to provide safe working conditions and fair wages. During the late 1990s certain businesses also actively cooperated with political leaders to shape more universal standards for workers' rights.

Recent Strides in Anti-sweatshop Legislation

The U.S. Congress is currently reviewing the Decent Working Conditions and Fair Competition Act. If signed into law, this act will ban the U.S. import, export, or sale of any items produced through sweatshop labor. Though the bill has yet to be incorporated into national legislation, it has support from both major political parties in the Senate and the House of Representatives.

Facts about the FLA

Thanks largely to the efforts of the Apparel Industry Partnership (AIP), the Fair Labor Association (FLA) was formally founded in 1999. This group is a collection of apparel companies, nonprofit organizations, and colleges and universities. Members have collaborated to further improve workplace standards on an international scale and to educate members of the public about the realities of sweatshop labor so they can make responsible decisions as consumers. The AIP attempts to strengthen communication between labor unions and employers so that workers have adequate representation and corporate decision makers are consistently aware of workers' needs.

In 1996 President Bill Clinton met with representatives from Liz Claiborne, Nike, Phillips-Van Heusen, and L.L. Bean, as well as various labor unions and human rights, religious, and consumer groups. Over the next few years the government-sponsored organization AIP established workplace codes that tackled issues including child labor, forced labor, discrimination, and excessive work hours. In addition, businesses that follow these codes are encouraged to hire outside parties to monitor their manufacturing centers. This external monitoring helps ensure that inspectors are dedicated to protecting laborers' rights, as opposed to being automatically biased toward company welfare, as is frequently the case with inspectors who are hired internally.

In addition, nonprofit organizations such as UNITE HERE, the International Labor Rights Forum (ILRF), and United Students Against Sweatshops (USAS) are all part of the crusade to eradicate sweatshops and to make average consumers aware of their existence. By necessity, businesses have to examine dollars and cents and the proverbial bottom line. Shoppers play an enormous role in the success of businesses and therefore in the way business leaders view the policies that spark public outrage.

From Store Shelves to Consumers' Consciences

"I search for 'sweat-free' labels when I buy products," says Heather Overdorf, a twenty-eight-year old mother who lives near Chicago, Illinois. "I look at it as a small thing I can do that doesn't take much time. But purchasing items from companies who care about workers' rights and human rights in general is nonetheless something that makes me

Members of UNITE!, a group that supports unions in the effort to end sweatshops, protest working conditions at The Gap factories.

feel like I'm helping to create better working conditions and, consequently, a better world."

The labels Overdorf references often feature the labels "UNITE," "UFCW: A Voice for Working America," "RUGMARK," or "Fair Trade Certified." Each signifies that workers who made the product in question were either represented by a union or employed by a manufacturer that demonstrated a commitment to opposing sweatshop labor.

Trina Tocco is a campaigns coordinator for the ILRF. She states that, in addition to searching for these labels, consumers can make several other simple, everyday decisions that go a long way toward ending human suffering in sweatshops.

> Ask questions and request information from retailers about [where] clothing is produced. This can be as easy as walking into ten stores at the mall as an average shopper and taking the time to ask . . . how they can assure the products aren't being made in a sweatshop. You can also support and participate in campaigns that bring about systematic change. Examples are college students focusing on [the source of] goods that bear their school logo or a community group working to pass a policy concerning the standards for police uniform production. You can even promote change the next time you're simply in a crowded room of people. Think about asking the person beside you how much they know about where their clothing comes from. . . . It's a great way to educate others about the issue.

From U.S. presidents intent on policy innovations to ordinary men and women looking to buy a shirt, it seems obvious that the global community is determined to eradicate sweatshops. Yet this goal will only be accomplished when more businesses subscribe to international codes that support laborers' rights and more consumers force politicians and

One way to support garment workers' rights is to search for clothing labels that indicate manufacturers support of unions and nonsweatshop labor.

industry leaders to realize that the public won't financially endorse institutions that do not. What part, however, will the flames of 1911 play in this effort? Will future generations perceive the lessons learned from the fire as a reminder of why history cannot afford to continually repeat itself, or will they merely view the inferno and its martyrs *as* history?

The Role of the Flames Nearly One Hundred Years Later

In February 2001, 107-year-old Rose Freedman died, and the last survivor of the Triangle Shirtwaist Factory fire was gone. Speaking of her experiences related to the blaze, Freedman once said, "That's the whole trouble of this fire. Nobody cares. Nobody. Hundred forty-six people in a half an hour. I have always tears in my eyes when I think. It should never have happened.... It's not fair because material, money is more important here than everything. That's the biggest mistake—that a person doesn't count much when he hasn't got money. What good is a rich man [when] he hasn't got a heart? I don't pretend. I feel it. Still."

It is incorrect to assume that twenty-first-century citizens cannot empathize with Freedman's feelings. Whether in Bangladesh or in any other country where sweatshops continue to operate, workers are forced to choose between their lives and their livelihoods on a daily basis. Dirnbach of UNITE HERE hopes the disaster of 1911 will force people to realize that labor rights have come a long way but that major strides still have to be made.

"The Triangle fire will always be remembered as a sweatshop tragedy that led to workplace improvements," he explains, "but unfortunately there are still many problems. Just as at Triangle, too many workers in the United States and around the world have to work in unsafe factories every day. There are industrial disasters every year that kill or injure workers. Triangle is a reminder of the past and how much things have improved since then, but it is also a reminder that much remains to be done."

The Triangle Shirtwaist Factory Fire

Besides its living legacy of labor rights, the fire is immortalized in countless books, annual commemorative ceremonies, poems, stories, theatrical productions, films, and songs. The following ballad by Ruth Rubin, a scholar who collects Yiddish folk songs, is one particularly stirring example:

> In the heart of New York City, near Washington
>   Square
> In nineteen eleven, March winds were cold and
>   bare.
> A fire broke out in a building ten stories high,
> And a hundred and forty-six young girls in those
>   flames did die.
>
> On the top floor of that building, ten stories in
>   the air
> These young girls were working in an old
>   sweatshop there;
> They were sewing shirtwaists for a very low wage.
> So tired and pale and worn-out! They were at a
>   tender age.
>
> The sweatshop was a stuffy room with but a single
>   door;
> The windows they were gray with dust from off
>   that dirty floor;
> There were no comforts, no fresh air, no light to
>   sew thereby,
> And the girls, they toiled from early morn till
>   darkness filled the sky.

Then on that fateful day — dear God, most terrible
    of days!
When that fire broke out, it grew into a mighty
    blaze.
In that firetrap way up there with but a single door,
So many innocent working girls burned, to live no
    more!

All the "innocent working girls burned" became powerful catalysts that raised public awareness. The victims aided
laborers from New York City to the far reaches of the world.
The knowledge of how and why they died has moved people
from many countries and walks of life. More important, it
has inspired society to realize that wealth and poverty, good
and evil, and guilt and innocence are complicated concepts,
but the need for adequate labor rights is a simple reality.

Timeline

1800   Social reformer Wirt Sikes notes the toll strenuous labor and poor working conditions take on female employees in a factory he tours.

1870–1900   Almost 12 million immigrants arrive in the United States; for more than 70 percent, New York City is the point of entrance.

1900   The ILGWU is formed; it is the first union to be comprised mainly of women.

1901   Construction is completed on the Asch Building at Greene Street and Washington Place in New York City.

1902   Blanck and Harris open the Triangle Shirtwaist Factory on the ninth floor of the Asch Buiding. By 1908 they occupy the eighth and tenth floors as well.

1909–1910   Approximately 20,000 New Yorkers in the shirtwaist trade, including Triangle laborers, participate in strikes known as the Uprising of 20,000.

1911   Fire erupts at the Triangle Shirtwaist Factory on March 25, resulting in the deaths of 146 workers. Blanck and Harris are indicted on charges of first- and second-degree manslaughter on April 11.

Jury selection gets underway the following December, and the accused are acquitted on December 27. New York State institutes the FIC, which ultimately inspects 1,836 factories, interviews 222 witnesses, and helps craft new safety and labor laws between 1911 and 1914. The commission inevitably turns its attention beyond the dilemmas that plague the garment industry. Members also examine conditions in businesses that involve baking, tobacco, printing, chemicals, and countless other types of manufacturing; The Sullivan-Hoey Law is passed in October and effectively leads to the establishment of the Bureau of Fire Prevention.

1912   Labor legislation is passed that stipulates that women employees not return to factories any earlier than four weeks subsequent to childbirth

1913   The U.S. DOL, officially set apart from the U.S. Department or Commerce, is formally established.

1914   Blanck and Harris settle twenty-three individual civil suits related to the fire at seventy-five dollars per life lost. The *New York Times* reports that the efforts of the FIC are driving manufacturers out of the city because of their stringent and sudden impact on labor statutes.

1920 Blanck and Harris dissolve their partnership.

1935 The National Labor Relations Act, which gives laborers the right to form unions, is passed.

1938 The Fair Labor Standards Act, which outlaws sweatshop production, is passed.

1970s U.S. apparel employment peaks and steadily declines thereafter, as a globalized economy takes root during the 1980s and 1990s.

1996 A report by the DOL states that about half of U.S. garment shops are in serious violation of wage and safety laws. President Clinton spearheads the formation of the AIP. TV personality and apparel producer Kathie Lee Gifford responds to allegations regarding her company's use of sweatshop labor.

1997 The DOL reports that about 67 percent of garment factories in New York City do not adhere to federal legislation regulating minimum wages and work hours.

1999 Thanks largely to the efforts of the FLA, the Fair Labor Association is founded.

2001   Rose Freedman, the last survivor of the Triangle Shirtwaist Factory fire, dies in February at age 107.

2006   A factory fire in Bangladesh on February 24 kills more than fifty people and injures about one hundred. It is reported that locked doors played a role in the tragedy.

2007   The U.S. Congress reviews the Decent Working Conditions and Fair Competition Act, which, if signed into law, will ban the U.S. import, export, or sale of any items produced through sweatshop labor.

Notes

Chapter One

p. 10, "men pouring water on the fire at the cutting tables . . .":
Sylvia Riegler, quoted by Leon Stein, *The Triangle Fire*,
Philadelphia: J. B. Lippincott, pp. 39–40.

p. 12, "no attempt at ventilation. The room is crowded . . .":
Wirt Sikes, "Among the Poor Girls," *The Triangle
Factory Fire: Documents*. 13 March 2007. Kheel Center
for Labor-Management Documentation and
Archives, Cornell University/ILR. http://www.ilr
.cornell.edu/trianglefire/texts/stein_ootss/ootss
_ws.html?location=Sweatshops+and+Strikes.
(Accessed March 27, 2008.)

p. 15, "never knew. For them, there was no fixed rate. They
got whatever . . .": Joseph Fletcher, quoted by Leon
Stein, *The Triangle Fire*, p. 161.

p. 19, "that individual protest amounted to the loss of
one's job . . .": Pauline Newman, "Letters to Michael
and Hugh from P. M. Newman," *The Triangle Factory
Fire: Documents*. http://www.ilr.cornell.edu/trianglefire/
texts/letters/newman_letter.html. (Accessed March 27,
2008.)

Chapter Two

p. 27, "she smelled something burning. . . . I looked to the
cutting tables . . .": Joseph Granick, quoted by Leon
Stein, *The Triangle Fire*, p. 34.

p. 27, "burning fabric began to fly around the room . . .": Max Rothen, quoted by Leon Stein, *The Triangle Fire*, p. 34.

p. 29, "the window of the elevator door with my hands . . .": Irene Seivos, quoted by Leon Stein, *The Triangle Fire*, p. 37.

p. 29, "so intense it was impossible to stand up . . .": Captain Howard Ruch, quoted by Leon Stein, *The Triangle Fire*, p. 42.

p. 29, "didn't seem to know which way to turn . . .": Edward N. Markowitz, quoted by Leon Stein, *The Triangle Fire*, p. 45.

p. 32, "didn't have a chance. The people on the eighth floor . . .": Rose Glantz, quoted by Leon Stein, *The Triangle Fire*, pp. 54–55.

p. 33, "back into the building. I still had one . . .": Abe Gordon, quoted by Leon Stein, *The Triangle Fire*, p. 58.

p. 35, "no picture to the imagination to say that the fire . . .": Charles Willis Thompson, "From the Charles Willis Thompson Letters, Rare and Manuscript Collections, Cornell University Library, Ithaca, NY," *The Triangle Factory Fire: Documents*. (Accessed March 27, 2008.)

p. 36, "first opened the elevator door on the ninth floor . . .": Joseph Zito, quoted by Leon Stein, *The Triangle Fire*, p. 62.

p. 39, "impression when I got down there and looked . . ." Charles Willis Thompson, The Triangle Factory Fire: Documents. http://www.ilr.cornell .edu/ trianglefire/texts/letters/dearwm_letter.html. (Accessed March 27, 2008.)

Chapter Three

p. 41, "to fit somebody; who is he?": from *The New York Evening Journal*, quoted by Leon Stein, *The Triangle Fire*, p. 114.

p. 42, "that the victims of this terrible catastrophe were poor working people . . .": Representative of the ILGWU, quoted by Leon Stein, *The Triangle Fire*, pp. 123–124.

p. 44, "the hard facts that will confront these bereaved . . .": Charles L. Slattery, quoted by Leon Stein, *The Triangle Fire*, pp. 134–135.

p. 45, "so constructed as to open outwardly . . . and shall not be locked, bolted . . .": Section 80 of New York State Labor Law (as cited by Max D. Steuer in 1911), "Summation of Max D. Steuer for the Defense in the Triangle Shirtwaist Fire Trial," *Famous Trials: The Triangle Fire Shirtwaist Trial — 1911*. 2002. The University of Missouri — Kansas City School of Law. http://www.law.umkc.edu/faculty/projects/ftrials/ triangle/steuersumm.html. (Accessed March 27, 2008.)

p. 45, "with our limited number of inspectors, to make regular . . .": Albert Ludwig, quoted by Leon Stein, *The Triangle Fire*, p. 116.

p. 46, "Labor Department has no supervision in the matter of fire escapes . . .": W. W. Walling, quoted by Leon Stein, *The Triangle Fire*, p. 114.

p. 48, "the golden era in remedial factory legislation": "The Triangle Shirtwaist Factory Fire Trial," *Famous*

Trials: The Triangle Fire Shirtwaist Trial—1911. http://
www.law.umkc.edu/faculty/projects/ftrials/triangle
/triangleaccount.html. (Accessed March 27, 2008.)

p. 48, "be a traitor to these poor burned bodies if . . .": Rose
Schneiderman, "We Have Found You Wanting," *The
Triangle Factory Fire: Documents.* http://www.ilr.cornell
.edu/trianglefire/texts/stein_ootss/ootss_rs.html.
(Accessed March 13, 2007.)

p. 49, "Murderers! Murderers!": "The Triangle Shirtwaist
Fire Trial: A Chronology," *Famous Trials: The Triangle
Fire Shirtwaist Trial—1911.* http://www.law.umkc.edu/
faculty/projects/ftrials/triangle/trianglechrono.html.
(Accessed March 27, 2008.)

p. 51, "locked up about six girls, and we found . . .": Isaac
Harris, quoted by Leon Stein, *The Triangle Fire*, p. 202.

p. 52, "The door was locked.": Anna Gullo, quoted by Leon
Stein, *The Triangle Fire*, p. 188.

p. 52, "I pushed at the door, and it would not open.": Ida
Nelson, quoted by Leon Stein, *The Triangle Fire*, p. 188.

p. 52, "be satisfied from the evidence . . . not merely that the
door was locked . . .": Thomas C. T. Crain, quoted by
Leon Stein, *The Triangle Fire*, p. 198.

p. 53, "see that anyone was responsible for the disaster. It
seems . . .": H. Houston Hierst, quoted by Leon Stein,
The Triangle Fire, p. 199.

p. 53, "have been tired out. Their money and their patience
have been exhausted . . .": from *The World*, quoted by
Leon Stein, *The Triangle Fire*, p. 207.

Chapter Four

p. 55, "a stricken conscience of public guilt, and we all felt . . .":
Frances Perkins, quoted by Leon Stein, *The Triangle
Fire*, p. 212.

p. 57, "for buildings include the Tenement House Department;
the Factory Inspection Department . . .": Edward
L. Croker, quoted by Leon Stein, *The Triangle Fire*, p. 121.

p. 58, "our industries were found housed in palatial loft
buildings . . .": Factory Investigating Commission,
"Results of the Data Obtained by the Investigation,"
The Triangle Factory Fire: Documents. http://www.ilr.
cornell.edu/trianglefire/texts/reports/nyfic_1912
_p128.html#LACK. (Accessed March 27, 2008.)

p. 62, "torch that lighted up the industrial scene.": Frances
Perkins, "New York State Factory Investigating
Commission Preliminary, Second, Third, and Fourth
Reports," *Women Working, 1800–1930*. 23 Aug. 2005.
Open Collections Program: Harvard University
Library. http://www.dol.gov/oasam/programs/history/
mono-regsafepart07.htm. (Accessed March 27, 2008.)

p. 63, "illustration of the present mercantile and factory
real estate conditions in New York . . .": George W.
Olvany, "The Fire Hazards in Big Buildings," The New
York Times, 3 May 1914. The *New York Times* Online
Archives. http://query.nytimes.com/mem/archive-free
/pdf?res=9D06E5D71E39E633A25750C0A9639C9465
96D6CF. (Accessed March 27, 2008.)

p. 64, "put property rights above life. The workers have a right to life . . .": William J. White, quoted by Leon Stein, *The Triangle Fire*, p. 142.

p. 67, "to foster, promote, and develop the welfare of working people . . .": "DOL Annual Report, Fiscal Year 2007," Performance and Accountability Report. U.S. Department of Labor. http://www.dol.gov/_sec/media/reports/annual2007/MDA.htm. (Accessed March 27, 2008.)

p. 67, "protecting [job seekers', wage earners', and retirees'] retirement and healthcare benefits . . . : "DOL Annual Report, Fiscal Year 2007." http://www.dol.gov/_sec/media/reports/annual 2007/MDA.htm. (Accessed March 27, 2008.)

Chapter Five

p. 68, "fifty people have been killed and about 100 injured in a fire at a textile mill in Bangladesh . . ." "Dozens Killed in Bangladesh Blaze," *One-Minute World News*. 24 Feb 2006. The British Broadcasting Corporation. http://news.bbc.co.uk/2/hi/south_asia/4745894.stm. (Accessed March 27, 2008.)

p. 68, "employment peaked in the 1970s and has declined ever since . . .": Interview with Eric Dirnbach, uniform Coordinator, UNITE HERE, March 5, 2008.

p. 69, "out of 22,000 U.S. garment shops, at least half were in serious violation . . .": Peter Liebhold and Harry

Rubenstein, "Between a Rock and a Hard Place: A History of American Sweatshops, 1820–Present," *History Matters: The U.S. Survey Course on the Web*. 31 March 2006. The American Social History Project/Center for Media and Learning (Graduate Center, CUNY) and the Center for History and New Media (George Mason University). http://historymatters.gmu.edu/d/145. (Accessed March 27, 2008.)

p. 71, "really don't like about this job is that it makes it difficult to . . ." Myra Esperanza Mejia, "A Fifteen-Year-Old Guatemalan Sweatshop Worker Explains."

p. 72, "If I didn't need to work, I would be in school.": Myra Esperanza Mejia, "A Fifteen-Year-Old Guatemalan Sweatshop Worker Explains—Why I Can't Lose My Job," *Jinn Magazine*. 18 Apr. 1997. Pacific News Service. http://www.pacificnews.org/jinn/stories/3.08/970418-maquila.html. (Accessed March 27, 2008.)

p. 74, "bell finally rings at 6:30 P.M., you are ready to go home . . ." Myra Esperanza Mejia, "A Fifteen-Year-Old Guatemalan Sweatshop Worker Explains."

p. 74, "helpless against the power of the exploiters": Pauline Newman, "Letters to Michael and Hugh from P. M. Newman," *The Triangle Factory Fire: Documents*. http://www.ilr.cornell.edu/trianglefire/texts/letters/newman_letter.html. (Accessed March 27, 2008.)

p. 78, "They'd hit us. They'd throw clothes at us.": Wendy Diaz, quoted in "Live with Kathie Lee and Apparel

Workers," The New York Times, 31 May 1996. The *New York Times* Online Archives. http://query.nytimes. com/gst/fullpage.html?res=9A04EFDB1E39F932A0575 6C0A960958260. (Accessed March 27, 2008.)

p. 78, "of the sweatshop should have been buried generations ago": Kathie Lee Gifford, quoted in "Live with Kathie Lee and Apparel Workers."

p. 79, "to return her work to the factory, but with better . . .": Wendy Diaz, quoted in "Live with Kathie Lee and Apparel Workers."

Chapter Six

p. 83, "for 'sweat-free' labels when I buy products. . .": Interview with Heather Overdorf, an average consumer, March 24, 2008.

p. 85, "and request information from retailers about [where] clothing is produced . . .": Interview with Trina Tocco, campaigns coordinator, International Labor Rights Forum, February 27, 2008.

p. 87, "whole trouble of this fire. Nobody cares. Nobody . . .": Rose Freedman, "Dedication to a Patriot for Worker Safety," *Letters: Rose Freedman.* Injured Workers' Alliance. http://www.injuredworker.org/Letters/Rose_ Freedman.htm. (Accessed March 27, 2008.)

p. 87, "will always be remembered as a sweatshop tragedy that led to workplace improvements . . .": Interview

with Eric Dirnbach, uniform coordinator, UNITE
HERE, March 5, 2008.

p. 88, "heart of New York City, near Washington Square,
In nineteen eleven, March . . .": Ruth Rubin, "Ballad of
the Triangle Fire," *The Triangle Factory Fire: Documents*.
http://www.ilr.cornell.edu/trianglefire/texts/songs/
ballad.html. (Accessed March 27, 2008.)

Further Information

Books

Haddix, Margaret Peterson. *Uprising.* New York: Simon & Schuster Children's Publishing, 2007.

Lieurance, Suzanne. *The Locket: Surviving the Triangle Shirtwaist Fire.* Berkeley Heights, NJ: Enslow Publishers, 2008.

Ross, Robert J. S. *Slaves to Fashion: Poverty and Abuse in the New Sweatshops.* Ann Arbor: University of Michigan Press, 2004.

Weber, Katharine. *Triangle.* New York: Farrar, Straus and Giroux, 2006.

DVD

The Triangle Factory Fire Scandal. Direct Source Label, 2006.

Websites

Global Exchange — Sweatfree Communities
www.globalexchange.org/campaigns/sweatshops
This site contains an overview of modern-day sweatshops, as well as information on the efforts to abolish them.

Kheel Center for Labor-Management Documentation and Archives
www.ilr.cornell.edu/trianglefire
This is a university-sponsored site with chronologies, primary documents, and eyewitness testimony related to the fire.

Bibliography

Books

Armbruster-Sandoval, Ralph. *Globalization and Cross-Border Labor Solidarity in the Americas: The Anti-Sweatshop Movement and the Struggle for Social Justice.* New York: Routledge, 2005.

Bender, Daniel E. *Sweated Work, Weak Bodies: Anti-Sweatshop Campaigns and Languages of Labor.* New Brunswick, NJ: Rutgers University Press, 2004.

Dolkart, Andrew S. *Biography of a Tenement House in New York City: An Architectural History of 97 Orchard Street.* Charlottesville: University of Virginia Press, 2006.

Ross, Robert J. S. *Slaves to Fashion: Poverty and Abuse in the New Sweatshops.* Ann Arbor: University of Michigan Press, 2004.

Stein, Leon. *The Triangle Fire.* Philadelphia: J. B. Lippincott, 1962.

Von Drehle, David. *Triangle: The Fire That Changed America.* New York: Grove/Atlantic, Inc., 2004.

Weber, Katharine. *Triangle.* New York : Farrar, Straus and Giroux, 2006.

Interviews

Interview with Eric Dirnbach, Uniform Coordinator, UNITE HERE, March 5, 2008.

Interview with Heather Overdorf, an average consumer, March 24, 2008.

Interview with Trina Tocco, Campaigns Coordinator, International Labor Rights Forum, February 27, 2008.

Websites

The American Social History Project/Center for Media and Learning (Graduate Center, CUNY) and the Center for History and New Media (George Mason University) — History Matters: The U.S. Survey Course on the Web: "Between a Rock and a Hard Place: A History of American Sweatshops, 1820–present" by Peter Liebold and Harry Rubenstein.
http://historymatters.gmu.edu/d/145

The British Broadcasting Corporation — One-Minute World News: "Dozens Killed in Bangladesh Blaze"
http://news.bbc.co.uk/2/hi/south_asia/4745894.stm

Injured Workers Alliance — Rose Freedman
http://www.injuredworker.org/Letters/Rose_Freedman.htm

Kheel Center for Labor-Management Documentation and Archives,Cornell University/ILR — The Triangle Factory Fire
http://www.ilr.cornell.edu/trianglefire/

The New York Times Online Archives — May 3, 1914
http://query.nytimes.com/mem/archive-free/pdf?res=9D06E
5D71E39E633A25750C0A9639C946596D6CF

The New York Times Online Archives — May 31, 1996
http://query.nytimes.com/gst/fullpage.html?res=9A04EFD
B1E39F932A05756C0A960958260

U. S. Department of Labor—The New York Factory Investigating Commission

http://www.dol.gov/oasam/programs/history/mono-regsafe part07.htm

The Pacific News Service—"A Fifteen-Year-Old Guatemalan Sweatshop Worker Explains—Why I Can't Lose My Job"

http://www.pacificnews.org/jinn/stories/3.08/97041 8-maquila.html

The University of Missouri–Kansas City School of Law—Famous Trials: The Triangle Shirtwaist Fire Trial—1911 by Douglas Linder.

http://www.law.umkc.edu/faculty/projects/ftrials/triangle /trianglefire.html

The U.S. Department of Labor—DOL Annual Report, Fiscal Year 2007, Performance and Accountability Report.

http://www.dol.gov/_sec/media/reports/annual2007/MDA .htm

Index

Page numbers in **bold face** are illustrations.

About the Author

KATIE MARSICO is the author of more than thirty reference books for children and young adults. Prior to becoming a full-time freelance writer, Marsico worked as a managing editor in publishing. She resides near Chicago, Illinois, with her husband and children.